DR. GOLDMANN

TRADING KING

how to become a millionaire

Ebozon Publishing

About the book

This book contains detailed successful trading strategies that can be proofed with original trading results of the broker and thus confirm that frequent profits with binary options are possible without any problems even out of your living room or office or any other place with an internet access.

Binary options trading can be a lucrative and highly profitable source of income for you.

With the right strategy and the necessary know-how, you can now proceed to make immediate profits. Trading novices learn in this book risk and return clearly to define and you also will learn everything you need to dominate the trade successfully.

You will get taught the basic knowledge of making money with trading binary options and how to place your first profitable trades and to secure high profits.

For beginners and experienced traders alike the author is offering online trading seminars or even entire trading sessions.

Trades placed with the author's strategy will achieve a verified average daily profit of about 2% of your trading capital. Do not miss out your chance to benefit from these profits right now!

Dr. Goldmann

Trading King

HOW TO BECOME A MILLIONAIRE

Ebozon Publishing

This book is also available as ebook.

4th edition August 2017
Paperback

a brand of CONDURIS UG (haftungsbeschränkt)
www.ebozon-verlag.com

Cover design: media designer 24
Cover graphics: Pixabay.com
Book design / layout: Ebozon Publishing
Print: KN Digitla Printforce GmbH,
Ferdinand-Jühlke-Straße 7, 99095 Erfurt

ISBN 978-3-95963-437-3

Table of contents

Binary options

What is a binary option?

A binary option, also known as a digital option or an all-or-nothing option, is one where the trader has two positions to decide between: will the value of an asset go up or will it go down over a set period of time? Depending on whether the trader is correct or not, the payout is a predetermined price or nothing.

For example, if a trader assumes a position that the value of gold will increase in a given period of time, and it is correct, he wins a fixed payout. If the value of gold drops however, the trader loses the entire amount of the investment. It does not matter if the asset exceeds the original price, the strike price, by $1 or $100: the payout is the same.

Binary Options are a new and exciting way to trade the financial markets. Prior to the introduction of online binary options trading, traders had to open accounts with brokers offering the currencies, commodities or stocks in the individual markets. So invariably, traders who wanted to trade all these assets had to create multiple accounts to do so. In 2008, an SEC (Securities and

Exchange Commission) ruling meant that binary options were no longer limited to being traded on an exchange. Online binary trading was born.

With online binary options trading, a trader can trade currencies, commodities, stock indices and stocks all from one trading platform. Trading online binary options aims to make money from taking a position in one of two possible outcomes. The trader only needs the outcome to be in his favour by just one pip to be able to make money. This is unlike other markets where profits earned are a direct consequence of the trade size and the number of pips gained.

What are the gains that online binary trading has to offer? Why is there so much noise about it in the marketplace?

1. Reduced Risk – Part of the appeal of online binary options trading is the reduced risk profile of this market. In other markets, traders have to contend with margin requirements, slippages and other broker or platform issues that affect the market outside the market conditions. In online binary trading, 80% of the traps that hurt all traders are all gone. No more stops, no more bad exits, and most of the bad emotions are gone!

2. Flexibility – The binary options market is a one-stop shop to trade financial assets across several asset classes. This means that traders are not stuck in one market. If a market is non-performing, the trader can simply switch to another asset. The trader can also choose between several trade types instead of the regular buy/sell trade mechanism.
3. Pay Structure – The pay structure of binary options trading is one that can give the trader magnified returns. For instance, a typical trade with an expiry of 10 minutes can give a trader up to $100. Such a short expiry allows the trader to effect this trade up to 10 times a day if need be. Even a success rate of 7 trades out of 10 would give the trader more returns than if the trader was in any other market. Of course in other markets, it is virtually impossible to get this same rate of return from many trades placed in a single day without taking excessive risk. With payouts of up to 80% on a single trade, the binary options market allows a trader to make profits that outperform profits on other markets when the risk factor to such trades are considered.
4. Accessible to All – Online binary options can be accessed by everyone. A typical ECN forex broker will demand $25,000 to open an account. A commodity or options broker will demand even more. Average

earners who can only afford small amounts for trading are therefore locked out. In contrast, a binary options trader can start with a much smaller amount, and can gradually build up his portfolio as he gains experience in the markets.

Although binary options are one of the simplest forms of financial trading, they cannot be traded successfully without you understanding the characteristics of their underlying assets or the impact of economic factors on their price. Therefore, it is essential that you and novice traders fully understand them before investing too much of your hard earned capital into your trading account.

Binary options give the novice trader a way to trade in multiple global markets such as the foreign exchange, stock, stock indices and commodities markets. Within these markets are hundreds of different types of assets. For example you can trade all the major currency pairs. This means that you have to know the characteristics and personality of the various currency pairs as well as the correlations between currency pairs and other assets.

Understanding the Correlations

If you know the correlations whether negative or positive between currencies and commodities, or currencies and currencies, or currencies and stock markets, or even stock markets and stock markets, your knowledge of binary options will increase and you will have far more success in your trading.

For example, if you knew that the EUR/USD and GBP/USD currency pairs had a strong positive correlation and you were fairly certain that the GBP/USD price would rise, as well as buying a GBP/USD call you could also buy a EUR/USD call. On the other hand EUR/USD and USD/CHF have a strong negative correlation, so if you were confident that for example the price of the EUR/USD currency pair was going down, you may wish to place a trade on the price of the USD/CHF currency pair rising. So you could buy a EUR/USD "Put" option, and a USD/CHF "Call" option.

Commodity Correlation

There are also currency correlations with commodities. For example, the price of gold is positively correlated with the AUD/USD currency pair. When the gold price rises, the price of the AUD/USD currency pair generally rises, as well. Meanwhile, the USD/CAD is negatively correlated with the price of oil. If the oil price increases so does the Canadian dollar. So if you were confident that oil prices were rising and you intended to buy an oil binary option "Call," you could also buy a USD/CAD "Put," as there is a very strong chance that the dollar would fall against the Canadian dollar.

Stock Indices Correlation

There are also correlations between stock indices such as the Dow Jones and the Nikkei which are positively correlated. So if you were confident that the Dow Jones index would rise you would buy a Dow Jones "Call," and, as the Nikkei index was positively correlated with the Dow Jones, you could also buy a Nikkei "Call" option. In addition, the Nikkei index is positively correlated with the USD/YEN currency pair so if you were confident that the Nikkei index was falling, you could buy a Nikkei "Put" option and buy a USD/YEN "Put" as well.

As you can see, the more you know about the underlying assets of binary options, their characteristics and their correlations, the better your chances of making very good profits.

Dispelling the Myths

Firstly, many people believe that trading binary options successfully is based on luck. This is not the case, although there are at times last minute extreme changes in prices. If you learn trading strategies you will be able to predict fairly accurately the price behaviour of an asset and thereby make a profit on your trades. You don't have to be a financial guru to trade binary options. If you have the correct approach binary option trading can be a wonderful method of increasing your income. You just need to be positive and want to spend time learning about the characteristics of binary trading. Binary options were designed to be traded as a simple investment route compared to the other conventional markets such as the foreign exchange and commodities markets.

Anyone can trade binary options, however, it's not for investors with a gambler's mentality. A trader with a gambler's mentality can lose a lot of money as all he does all day is mindlessly buy calls and puts. Predicting if the price of an asset is going to fall or rise within an hour is very exciting because in a moment the price can change due to economic news or some other information which can cause an asset to gain or lose in price.

Also many people think you need a lot of money to start trading options. This is also a myth. In reality, you can open an account with a respectable broker with very little money. You can open an account with as little as $250. Meanwhile, brokers don't ask you to pay commission fees either.

Most people think that trading binary options means sitting in front of your computer all day long buying or selling calls and puts and then being stressed out for days waiting for your option to expire while wondering if you predicted the right way or not. This is not the case as binary options are short term investments. So they are very short-term, stress-free, investments indeed.

Another popular myth is that before you start making money and become a successful trader, you must lose a lot of money while you are going through a trading learning curve. This is not true at all as a trade can be made on as little as $1, thereby allowing plenty of room for practice. In a nutshell binary option trading is simple and affordable and is fast becoming the investment of choice.

How to Choose a Broker

If you want to start investing in binary options, you will have to look for and choose an online broker that has a trading platform which supports binary options trading. A trading platform is a real-time trading system which is web-based, on which traders can conduct over the counter binary options trading.

There are many binary option brokers on-line, some of which are regulated and some of which are non-regulated. A regulated broker is a broker that follows the rules and regulations of the country in which it is based. For example a binary option broker in the United Kingdom could be regulated by the Financial Securities Authority (FSA). One of the key rules which regulated brokers have to follow is to use a trust account for holding clients' money, whereas a non-regulated broker is not required to do that. This is not to say that you should not use non-regulated brokers as there are many that are perfectly safe to use, however, there are several criteria you should check out before making your decision as to which broker to use; whether it's an un-regulated broker, or a regulated broker.

1. Look for a broker that offers a variety of assets.

You should find a broker that offers many different types of options covering as many stocks, currencies, commodities and indices as possible. A large variety of option choices will enable you to be flexible and have a good range of profit opportunities.

2. Make sure your broker also offers a variety of expiry times.

Quality Binary Options brokers offer sixty seconds, ten minutes, fifteen minutes, half-hour, hourly, daily, weekly and even monthly expiry times.

3. Simplicity and Reliability come first!

Make sure that the trading platform is intuitive to use, responsive and the rates are true market rates. If the platform is complicated to use, you will find yourself making silly mistakes and losing money.

4. Great Customer Service is another must!

Fourthly, also make sure that the customer service and support is immediate and you can get help in a timely manner. Most broker web sites also have educational materials, which are designed to help new traders understand binary option trading concepts.

5. Quick and Secure Money Transfers.

Finally, a very crucial point concerns money and how the broker transfers funds in and out of your account. You will need to ensure that it is easy to deposit funds as well as withdraw funds to your credit card or bank account. Another thing that you should confirm is how their bonus schemes operate and the percentages of their pay-outs. One last thing you can do is to check out the broker reviews that are on the internet. Most of them are impartial and very helpful, and so will help you choose a broker you trust and feel comfortable trading on their platform.

How to Find a Trusted Broker?

With the emergence of new markets comes a large number of new brokers. Often unregulated, these binary options brokers are an unknown quantity and especially if you are new to trading in the financial markets, this can lead to confusion. Binary options trading can be extremely rewarding for professional traders and newcomers but you need to find a reputable broker to deal with and one who you can trust with your money.

This is one of the basic hurdles that you will need to overcome before you take the plunge into the exciting world of binary options trading. Bearing in mind that there is also a huge amount of information or misinformation that can be found on the internet posted by irate traders, and sometimes, competing brokers, how do you go about finding a reputable binary options broker when you are faced with a choice of hundreds of other firms?

One of the most important issues to consider when choosing a binary options broker and opening a trading account is whether they are regulated. For the binary options market, regulation will ensure that your funds are safe and that you are paid your trading profits accordingly.

The most reputable binary brokers will have usually obtained a trading license distributed by a financial oversight commission. Licenses are awarded to trustworthy brokers as many national governments are recognising binary options as a legitimate investment vehicle.

A license is essentially a contractual agreement stipulating that the broker must follow a series of rules and oversight regulations that ensure that traders can confidently and reliably use the services provided by the broker. These may include receiving withdrawals in timely fashion upon the client's request and ensuring an overall fair trading platform, including the integrity of price quotes. Breach of these regulations can result in fines, legal problems for the company's owners and revocation of their licenses.

To reiterate, it is recommended that as a binary options trader you should find a broker that has a license from an oversight commission for your own safety and to limit the chance of becoming a potential victim of fraud and general business misconduct. With some level of regulation now increasingly common in the industry, you should do business only with regulated brokers.

Binary options trading has regulation in several jurisdictions with reputable financial oversight commissions. Here is a list: United States/ *Commodity Futures Trading Commission* (CFTC), United Kingdom/Financial Conduct Authority (FCA), Cyprus/Cyprus Securities and Exchange Commission (CySEC), Japan/Japan Financial Services Agency (JFSA), South Africa/Financial Services Board (FSB), Belize/International Financial Services Commission (IFSC) and Malta/Malta Financial Services Authority (MFSA).

Top Brokers

In general there are only a few „black sheeps“ out of hundreds of brokers worldwide. Therefore, if you start trading with a regulated and licensed broker you should not face any problems at all. I can only promote such brokers that I am trading myself with. My favorite broker here is by far

24 Option: http://option.go2jump.org/SHxUMN

However, this broker stoped trading binary options for new clients and will now only offer CFD and Forex trading. If you are interested in these trading methods I highly can recommend you 24 Options. Further I made very good experiences with IQ-Option, 365trading.com and Stockpair.

Binary Options Common Terms

Fortunately you don't need a math degree to start trading binary options, or '**digital options**', which is the alternative name for them, and nor do you need an amazing memory to learn the common place terms you will come across when you start trading.

The most common term of all is the collective name for what you are going to trade. You can trade a commodity, maybe gold, or oil, or even copper. You can also trade the individual stocks of well-known companies such as Facebook, Apple or McDonalds; you can trade stock indices like the NASDAQ, S&P 500 or FTSE 100, or you can trade a currency pair such as the EUR/USD or GBP/USD. These are collectively called '**assets**', so the asset is the item that you are trading.

Let's assume you want to trade the currency pair EUR/USD and the price at the moment is 1.2900, this is called the '**market price**'. You decide to read one of the financial newspapers to see if there is any economic news that will be published today that might affect the price of the pair. This is called conducting '**fundamental analysis**'. If you had decided to browse through historical price charts of the EUR/USD currency pair to identify historical chart price patterns you would be conducting '**technical analysis**'.

After your research, you conclude that the price of the EUR/USD will move higher, so you decide to buy a '**call option**' at a price of your choosing (1.2910) which is higher than the market price of 1.2900. This price is termed the '**strike price**', and the time when the option expires is termed the '**expiry time**'.

If you had concluded that the price of the EUR/USD would move lower, you would have purchased a '**put option**' and chosen a strike price which was lower than the market price of 1.2900, (say 1.2890).

Now you wait and watch. Are you going to predict correctly or not? The EUR/USD price doesn't move at all at first and you are not making a profit or thank goodness a loss on the deal. This situation is called being '**at-the-money**', and if the price at expiry was at-the-money, you would break even. However, the price starts to move quite rapidly and is quite volatile. Initially it falls to 1.2885, and you become agitated because now the option is '**out-of-the-money**', and if the price remains where it is you will make a loss on the transaction and lose your initial '**investment amount**'.

However, as time passes the price of the EUR/USD starts to climb and moves above 1.2910 which is your strike price. Now you are happy because your call option is deemed to be '**in-the-money**', and you are going to get a nice '**pay-out**' and make a nice hefty profit on the transaction, about 71% of your investment amount. Not bad eh?

Learn How To Trade

Although this may seem obvious, many new traders jump into trading without fully understanding how to trade and end up losing their funds. It is important to educate yourself and take advantage of the broker's demo system to practice trading, while testing out strategies that you may consider using when live trading.

Choose A Reputable Binary Options Broker

Look for a licensed broker with a wide choice of assets and a high rate of payout. There are many new brokers appearing on the market every day, many of whom will not yet have gained a reputation. It is, therefore vital that you choose an established broker that is governed by the appropriate financial oversight commission.

Research The Markets And Implement A Strategy

Successful traders research their assets well while keeping up to date with any news that is likely to affect their asset price by checking what events are coming up that may cause the asset price to rise or fall. In addition, they use proven strategies and tools that work for them. Trading without research or a reliable binary options trading strategy is a guaranteed way to lose more trades than you win.

Manage Your Money And Your Risks

It is important that as a trader, you "don't put all your eggs in one basket". You should never risk too much of your capital on one trade. Many traders never risk more than 5% of their capital on a single trade. If it goes wrong they will still have a sizable portion of their capital available to continue and can recover quickly.

Keep Emotions Aside And Don't Expect To Get Rich Quick

Dealing with your money is no place to be emotional. Emotional decisions often transform decisions to a game of luck. Many new traders make emotional decisions after a loss and immediately place a bid for the next option to "cut losses". Accepting losses and "picking yourself up" before the next bid is the right way to act. Follow this rule in your first steps and you will save yourself from large losses. You should always be realistic about wealth potential and understand that you only get out what you put in.

While these tips are not a guarantee of instant success they will help you fine tune your trading skills and give you some guidance on the best way to maximise your profit potential.

Trader's Guide to Binary Options Trading Platforms

Enhancing Trading Success via Trading Platforms!

The worldwide popularity of binary options trading has sparked tremendous interest among traders regarding the attributes of binary options platforms. At their very core, binary options are digital options, or fixed return options. One of the leading binary options brokers 24 Option provides traders with a fully functional, robust and user-friendly trading platform. The benefits of trading options are many, including the fact that these all or nothing options have only one possible outcome.

Traders can either enjoy profits or losses. If the option ends in the money, traders profit, while the converse holds true too. These are a preferred trading option for many investors since losses are limited to the contract value of the chosen commodity. Regardless of the tradable asset selected, the most important criterion is the selection of the binary options platform. The majority of online traders prefer web-based trading platforms that offer one quick click access to the worldwide markets.

Binary Trading Platform Options

There are 4 commonly traded assets with binary options. These include stocks, indices, commodities and currencies. As a case in point, 24 Option provides traders with real-time charts and trading graphics that range from 30 min – one hour – two hours – four hours – eight hours – 12 hours. Traders can customize their market analysis based on these time intervals. Among the most popular currency pairs are the following: EUR/USD (up or down), USD/JPY (up or down), and AUD/USD (up or down). Of course, scores of other currency options are available to traders, but the essence of a binary options trading platform is the same. Traders simply decide whether to place a call option or a put option. A call option is for traders feeling bullish about the future expected value of the currency, while a put option is for traders feeling bearish about the future expected value. The easy-to-use functionality on site instantly provides traders with an expected payout percentage (typically 70% or higher) and the potential payout amount. As a case in point, traders can bet on the currency pairs (or other assets) and forecast the future payout percentage. It is important to choose the amount and the expiry time for each specific asset that has been selected. Binary options trading platforms provide 4 investment options.

It is important to choose a binary options trading platform that offers you returns in the region of 65% to 70% at minimum. Note that you will always know your potential payout percentage in advance with binary options, unlike other investment opportunities which can incur large potential losses. With binary options contracts, traders are paid a fixed return – regardless of the value of the price movement. In other words, the only thing that is important with binary options trading is the direction of movement – not the value that it moved. Returns in the region of 65% to 70% at minimum should only be considered. In the absence of such returns, the risk/reward ratio is simply not worth the effort. If possible, it's always a good idea to select a binary options trading platform that provides payback for options that expire out of the money. This is a rarity, but it is certainly a boon if you can find one. Of paramount importance to any serious or intending binary options trader is the selection of a platform supporting multiple currencies. Variety certainly is the spice of life, and so it is true with a binary trading platform. As mentioned earlier, the most important currencies that need to be supported are the Great British Pound, the Euro, the US Dollar, the Australian Dollar, the Canadian Dollar, Japanese Yen and others.

Safety and Security are Paramount

All reputable and regulated binary options trading providers provide 100% safety and security for all traders. The integrity of all trader information should be watertight at all times. At minimum, secure socket layer encryption (SSL technology 128 bit) and advanced security protocols are a requirement. Additionally 24/7, 5 days a week customer support is a valuable option. Binary options trading providers with technical support services certainly warrants careful consideration over others. In addition to a wide range of safe and secure deposit options, traders need to ensure that they can withdraw their funds safely, securely and easily. A binary options trading platform that does not support easy withdrawals of funds is not worth considering. Check the terms and conditions associated with your preferred binary options broker before you deposit funds.

Web-Based Platforms

These are the traditional binary trading platforms that are used on the binary options market. Every binary options broker offers web-based platforms. There are basically four different trading platform solutions used in the market presently. They are as follows:

- SpotOption
- Tech Financials
- Tradologic
- Proprietary platforms

The SpotOption trading platform has the widest use in the market. This is the trading platform used by brokers such as iOption, TradeRush, Zoomtrader, Dragon Options, Option365, OptionClick, Fonbet, Ikko Trader, etc. It is on this platform that 60 second options were first introduced to traders. Other trade types offered on SpotOption are the conventional Call/Put options (also known as Up/Down) and the High Yield Touch option. Range binary options are not offered on Spot Option.

Tech Financials Ltd's binary trading platform is unique in that it has a plug-in for the MetaTrader4 platform, which is an industry first. The Tech Financials trading platform is used by brokers such as OptionFair and 24Option. Traders using the Tech Financials platform can trade the In/Out range option, the High/Low option and the Touch/No Touch. Given the increased popularity of the 60 seconds option, this has also been added to the product offering.

Tradologic's BINARIX™ trading platform is used by brokers such as RTOption, BinaryWinner, Almishal Trading, OptionBit, GFMTrader and OptionXP. This binary trading platform offers the One Touch, Touch Up/Down In/Out and Digital Call/Put options.

Proprietary platforms are custom-made binary trading platforms which the brokers have designed for themselves according to their own requirements and trade contracts that they offer traders. Sometimes a broker may design its own trade types which are distinct from what obtains on the white-label platforms mentioned above. This is where proprietary platforms come into play. Betonmarkets and Saxo Bank are two binary options brokers who feature proprietary platforms.

Mobile-Based Binary Trading Platforms

With the advent of the smartphones in 2007, companies realised a solution to an age-old problem that traders had, that of portability. With a desktop or laptop, it was impossible to trade on the go. Traders had no true chance to check positions while out for dinner, travelling or even on the golf course. The design and production of trading applications built specifically for the smartphones gave traders access to a fully portable solution to enable binary trading anywhere they went. Smartphones and tablet devices have become the wave of the future, as traders are dumping the traditional computers for these sleeker wonders of technology.

The only difference between the web-based platforms and the mobile versions is that the mobile versions are built specifically to adjust to the different environment that the smartphones and tablet devices offer. For instance, being able to adjust to the reduced screen sizes and still get a very good display is a major challenge that the trading applications for the iPhone, iPad, Android and Windows mobile devices have been able to surmount. Smartphone trading is now available with brokers like Saxo Bank, OptionFair and Betonmarkets. As the revolution catches on, we will see more brokers offering mobile platforms for trading.

Long Term Platform

This trading platform is a newcomer to the binary options market. As the platform's name suggests, Long Term options have a longer self-life than traditional binary options, with a choice of expiry dates ranging from one day, to several days, weeks, or even months. The longer expiry dates of these options, moreover, introduce a whole new way of trading and an array of trading techniques not previously available to binary options. With Long Term options, no longer does a trader have to depend solely on technical analysis of fleeting events and immediate shifts in the direction of the markets; they can now rely more heavily on global economic news and external factors that could influence the underlying asset. This means, however, that prior to entering a trade, one needs to understand why an expiry date is recommended and how to analyse the events leading up to it.

Long Term Options Strategies

One of the main advantages of trading Long Term options lies in the lesser degree of risk they offer, in comparison to other binary options. Although less risk brings with it a smaller profit potential, good analysis of events, paired with a strong investment strategy, can turn Long Term options into an important trading tool.

Seasonality: Any experienced trader will tell you that there are certain trends that repeat themselves in the market every year at the same period. Although there is no guarantee that a historical pattern will repeat itself in the same way, an 80-90% repetition rate makes such patterns a significant factor to monitor on the Long Term trading platform. For example, the price of oil can be seen peaking in August of each year on account of the higher demand placed on the market by the many holiday-makers of this month. An investor interested in oil, therefore, should keep this event in mind in deciding whether a Long Term trade in oil will go up or down by the expiry date.

Buy Low, Sell High & Vice Versa: The 'Buy Low, Sell High' strategy has been the driving force of the traditional stock market since its inception, and has not previously been applicable to binary options. With trading platforms such as Long Term, however, investors can not only apply this strategy to their trades, they can also from its inverse, 'Buy High, Sell Low'—an unthinkable notion for those dealing in the stock market. When a currency or a commodity hits a record low, for example, a trader could place a "call" Long Term option that closes at a later time when the market will have return to its normal range. The inverse also works in the binary market: when a value hits a record high, a Long Term "put" option for a later expiry date should catch the market at its return to normalcy and expire in-the-money.

60 Seconds Trading Platform

The 60 Seconds Trading Platform offers traders the fastest possible way to profit from online investments. This online trading platform works exactly like the regular binary options platform, in that the investor chooses which asset to trade, the direction of the asset's value, and the amount they would like to invest. The difference between the two platforms lies in the expiry time of the trade; in the 60 Seconds Platform the investor cannot choose the expiry time, as the trade is set to automatically expire in 60 seconds. At the end of the sixty seconds, a successful trade can yield profits of around 65-75% of the original investment amount, and can even be repeated for as long as the market trend continues.

Advantages of 60 Sec. Platform

The 60 Seconds trading platform may seem like a quick and easy way to make a profit, but it should be used with caution, as the fast turnaround of these trades requires prior knowledge of the market and a good understanding of the events that affect short-term movements. Using this trading platform, traders can capitalise on the volatility of the market preceding major economic data releases, such as the NFP.

60 Seconds Trade Using the NFP

The American Non-Farm Payroll report, or NFP, is a measure of the change in the number of employed people in the United States (excluding farm and government employees and people who work for non-profit organizations). The report is released on the first Friday of every month at 12.30 p.m. GMT and is one of the most important trading opportunities for binary options investors. The number of people in work is perhaps the best indicator of the strength of an economy. And because we measure economic strength through the tradable value of currencies, binary options investors can make big profits by taking advantage of the short-term NFP.

For example, on Friday May the 3rd 2013, the NFP forecast was for an increase of 146,000 employed Americans. This is positive news for the US economy – and the dollar – but beware. This estimate has already been priced into the currency markets. If the actual change in the number of unemployed Americans is 146,000 (or close to that number) there is no trading opportunity. What we are looking for is an actual figure that is significantly higher or lower than the estimate. At least 10,000 either way is a good benchmark. Just before 12.30 p.m. GMT, the interested investor should log into the 60 Seconds Trading Platform and prepare to trade in EUR/USD—the most liquid currency pair. A few seconds after 12.30 p.m. GMT the actual NFP number is published – it's 165,000. A positive change of 19,000 and very good news for the US dollar and binary options investors who can now invest on the temporarily falling EUR/USD currency pair as the USD rises in value.

Digital Options Pro

Digital Options Pro refers to the name of the standard binary options platform that most online brokers offer to their clients for placing trades. When you log into the homepage of most binary options broker, the Digital Options Pro Platform holds the main position on the page with its featured chart and "call" and "put" buttons. Familiarizing yourself with this platform and all its useful tools should be the first priority in your foray into the binary options trading world, for this platform will become the base of your trading career.

How to Use Digital Options Pro

Binary options trading provides you, the trader, a great gamut of assets to trade, giving you full control over the structure and content of your trading portfolio. The Digital Options Pro platform allows you to choose among currency pairs, stocks, indices, and commodities according to your personal preferences. Once you select an asset and study its chart, it's time to choose an expiry date for your trade from the list of options provided by the platform. The time-frame of your investment, whether short or long, depends on your estimates regarding price movements and the preference of your trading style. After you set an expiry time, you may enter the amount you would like to invest. On the Digital Options Pro platform you can see the return rate of your investment, typically between 70-80 percent, so you know exactly what to expect from all successful trades. Now, all that remains is to hit the "call" button, if you believe the price of your chosen asset will rise within your selected time-frame, or the "put" button, if you believe the price will fall. That's it! You're a trader!

The user-friendly interface of this platform and its ease of use attracts not only beginning traders, but also seasoned traders. The simplicity of the platform takes unnecessary guessing out of your trading strategy and allows you instead to focus on the parameters of your trade that really count: type of asset, expiry time, investment amount, and return rate. Mastering the Digital Options Pro platform, moreover, will allow you to understand the other binary options platform provided by your broker, all of which are variants of this basic one.

Pairs Trading Platform

Pairs trading is a strategy which enables traders to profit from virtually any market conditions; uptrend, downtrend or sideways movement. The pairs trade is market-neutral, meaning the direction of the overall market does not affect its win or loss.

Pairs trading works by monitoring the performance of two historically correlated securities, buying one stock and at the same time, short selling another correlated stock – then exiting the pair trade once the relationship between the two stocks has returned to its average. The divergence within a pair can be caused by temporary supply/demand changes, large buy/sell orders for one security or a reaction to important news about one of the companies for example. It has been a widely used trading system by professional traders and hedge funds all around the world for decades and its appeal is that it has the potential to achieve profits through simple and relatively low-risk positions.

When using a pairs trading system, you have to ensure you are trading two similar stocks. Coke/Pepsi is an example of a correlated pair. They are two very similar companies in that they both operate in the same markets and sell the same products; non-alcoholic beverages. As they are both exposed to the same macro-economic and industry conditions, their stock prices are priced with similar valuations by the market. Ebay/Amazon, commodities like Gold/Silver and Indices such as Dow Jones/FTSE are further examples of correlated pairs. You should always make sure your trading platform tells you the correlation between the two similar stocks is above 70% with really good pairs above 90% correlation.

If the pairs diverge away from each other, this represents a pairs trading opportunity to make money, so you would buy the asset that has gone down, short sell the asset that has gone up, and exit once the relationship between the two correlated stocks returns to normal. This is also known as reversion to the mean, statistical arbitrage, market neutral or long/short trading. By always having an equal amount of your account in long and short positions, this will keep your portfolio market neutral. In this way, you are not exposed to large one way market swings as you are betting on the relationship between two correlated pairs, not on the outright direction of the market. This significantly reduces your risk and allows you to safely increase your trading leverage.

The pairs trading strategy works with stocks as well as with currencies, commodities and binary options. Binary options traders use calls and puts to hedge risks and exploit volatility. A pairs trade in the binary options market might involve trading a call for an asset that is outperforming its pair and matching the position by trading a put for the pair. As the two underlying positions revert to their mean again, the options become worthless allowing the trader to pocket the proceeds from one or both of the positions.

Pairs trading has proved to be a very effective method for consistent profits. It has also increased in popularity mainly due to the advent of the internet and advancements in trading technology. This means that market participants now have access to real-time financial market data and advanced computer modeling. As there are 1000s of stock pairs out there to trade, it is impossible to calculate all of the correlations manually so you need to access a pairs trading platform in order to find the right pairs, which in turn will allow you to embark on a profitable pairs trading strategy.

What Are Trading Signals?

If you are new to trading, it is important that you make the right decisions. One wrong trading move can drastically harm your trading account while a good move can bring great profits. There are two key components which are necessary from the start: a combination of a winning equity management strategy and a well-planned trading system for whatever you are trading, whether it be forex, stocks, indices or commodities. The absence of these two factors will ultimately spell disaster for an investor or trader.

Signals: what exactly are they anyway?

A key feature that you need to have access to is trade alerts or "signals." Trading signals are very important. They are indicators that let you know when it's a good time to buy or sell an asset. They provide you with insight as to what's going on in the markets without the necessity to monitor trends throughout the day. What are trading signals? Normally referred to as entry and exit signals, they are the result of a vast amount of in-depth analysis, research and tracking that the different trading systems engage in on an ongoing basis.

Trading signal providers are available to provide signals around the clock. It is advisable to try a demo account first for practice so that you can create a strategy that works for you. You can then add trading signal services as a useful tool in your trading. Most brokers offer signal alert services, either themselves or through third party arrangements. If you trade either with a demo account or a real account the signal service is free.

Signals can be e-mailed or texted to your mobile phone, or you can simply visit the broker's website to get the signal. The services also vary in how they present information to you. Some will provide live charts to give you more insight and a head's up as to what is happening in the market. You can receive the signals, and then decide if you want to buy or sell.

This is a highly competitive arena so remember that a well-planned trading system and subscribing to a reputable broker with a signaling feature is paramount to your success or failure in the currency exchange market.

The following signal providers have been recommended by our readers:

Binary Signal Trader

http://host.robotclicks.com/click.php?project_id=2bn-&affiliate_id=Kt&affiliate_display=Kt

Signal Samurai

http://host.robotclicks.com/click.php?project_id=3bn-&affiliate_id=Kt&affiliate_display=Kt

Binary Copier

http://host.robotclicks.com/click.php?project_id=Ebn-&affiliate_id=Kt&affiliate_display=Kt

How to Use Trading Signals

Using signals is very important for traders. If a trader is interested in using signals in his trading, he has to ensure that they reach him quickly, and without delay.

The main function of trading signals is to assist traders to buy and sell profitably. They are a very important factor in that they provide a trader with the information required to enter and exit the markets. They are a vital insight as to what is happening in the markets without the need to monitor trends throughout the day.

Trading signals are normally referred to as entry and exit signals. They are the result of a vast amount of in-depth analysis, research and tracking that the different trading systems engage in on an ongoing basis. As well as learning how to use trading signals, it is also advisable to use trading signal services which can be accessed free of charge via a broker, although there are also some services which are available for a fee.

Signals for Assets

There is a different range of trading signals for assets available which are appropriate for each asset category. It is important to learn more about what they do in order to improve your results as you implement your trading strategy.

Market Signals

For any asset category, it is important to understand how sensitive its value can be to movements in the market. Historically, if an asset has been quick to react to the release of new economic data, it may be a signal of how it may react in the future. If for example, a trader recognizes that the value of the S&P 500 index has changed course following the release of key US economic indicators, such as the unemployment rate, this should be taken into consideration when attempting to determine the asset's price movement if similar data is released in the future.

Price/Value Trending Signals

It is also important to learn how prices move within a given period of time. The values of many assets appear to move in cycles and by observing the value over time, you can identify whether there are any trends related to changes in the asset's value. For example, the S&P 500 is largely influenced by the performance of its components i.e. the 500 largest US stocks. Since these components are publicly traded corporations they report results on a quarterly basis. If you are trading on the S&P 500 and you notice that there is a spike in its value a week before these releases, it may be a signal for a price/value trend for this asset.

Timing Signals

Since many markets are traded within a pre-defined set of trading hours, signals can exist as certain timeframes approach. For example, with the S&P 500 asset you may notice that the index has shown its biggest gains in the first 30 minutes of trading for the past few trading days. This signal could help you decide whether a call or put option is appropriate depending on when you place the trade and its expiration time.

Keeping in tune with the appropriate signals will teach you more about your chosen asset's performance and improve your overall trading results. Here are some useful observations relating to signals in each asset category.

Index Signals

Index signals tend to be oriented to short term investors although position traders may take a longer view. Generally, traders look for quick movements so the transaction length typically varies between 1 to 5 days.

Stocks Signals

With stocks it is important to analyze company fundamentals and sector situation in order to identify tendency depth. Graphs will help to determine the exact moment to take bullish or bearish positions in the company which usually will take longer to play out with wider movements, so the average length of the trades will be over 15 days.

Forex Signals

Forex is the most traded market in the world and volatility is usually very high, so the safest option is looking for quick movements. Transactions are usually opened and closed on the same day although swing traders will take longer term positions with wider stops.

Commodities Signals

These signals don't appear very often, but when they show they generate high profitability because of their tendency movements. At certain moments the volatility of commodities can be excessive and movements are very erratic. For example, the oil market which reacts instantly to unexpected news events.

How Signals Work?

As the two newcomers on the trading scene, forex and binary options are sometimes grouped together as online trading tools. These two platforms however present many differences in their mode of operation that we need to clarify before explaining the specific distinctions between their signals.

When trading in forex, you are speculating whether the price of an asset will increase or decrease as well as the degree of the projected change. When you feel confident about your speculation, you can enter the trade by buying options and waiting for the price to reach your predicted target before exiting the trade by selling. This requires a good amount of patience. With binary options, on the other hand, things are simpler. All you have to speculate is whether the price of an asset will rise or fall; the degree of the change does not concern the binary options trader. Once you have determined the direction of the price, you can place a "call" option for upwards-moving values, or a "put" option for downwards-moving ones. At the time you place your trade you also choose an expiry time, usually ranging between a few minutes to a few hours, and wait for your trade to close. If you predicted the direction of the movement correctly, your trade finishes in-the-money. It's as quick and simple as that.

Another major difference between forex and binary options is the degree of profits and losses. Although forex places no maximum cap on your profit, it also has no maximum limit for your losses; a trade turned sour can cost you a great amount of money which you may not be prepared to lose. Binary options, on the other hand, offered by reputable companies, have a fixed re turn rate – usually between 70 and 90 percent – which you know before you place your trade, and a limited loss equal to the original amount of your trade. The limited risk inherent in trading binary options makes them much more appealing and safe to most traders.

In terms of signals that alert traders to opportunities in the forex or the binary options market, a similar pattern emerges. Forex signals notify traders of good buys to be made on an asset at a specific date and time. These signals, however, offer no closing time at which you could realize your profit; instead you need to monitor the market patiently and wait for a good closing opportunity to appear, or be alerted by another signal about a potential payoff trade. On the contrary, binary option signals alert traders to opportunities on which they can capitalize within a short period of time. With the direction of the price within a specific time frame being the only variable in binary options trading, a signal can quickly generate a profitable trade for you if the price moves in the predicted direction by your trade's expiry.

Live Binary Options Signals

Some traders heavily rely on the use of binary options trading signals to place their trades. Binary options trading signals indicate the major events that can affect the market and show how a particular asset predicted to behave at a particular moment to help investors decide on how to place their trades. These signals are used by all kinds of traders: novice traders looking for advice and guidance on how to place trades, traders with little free time to follow the market movements prior to placing trades, and especially expert traders who analyse all details before making their investments and seek confirmation of their predictions from other sources. Live Binary Options Trading Signals can be beneficial and extremely helpful in deciding which trades to place in a given moment, making them an important tool for any trader to master. Such signals, however, are not infallible and should be taken as expert advice rather than guaranteed profit makers.

Many Binary Options Trading Platforms, offer investors a medley of live tools and updates they can use during trading, such as live price values, live charts recording value movements in real time, as well as daily trading signals delivered by email. Due to the time-sensitive nature of binary options, traders like to be updated on trading signals constantly, especially during a trading session.

With short expiry times of as little as 60 seconds, many consider it crucial that trading signals reach investors as close to the time of trading as possible, hence the creation of Live Binary Options Signals. Technological advancements have made the transmission of Live Binary Options Signals possible through such immediate means of communication as text messaging, live chat rooms and emails. Interested traders can subscribe to trading platforms and other services that allow them to follow current trading conditions and trends prior to placing their trades.

The savvy trader will naturally make use of all these tools to understand the movements in the market and the reasons driving certain expert predictions in order to gain an advantage on the market and place smart trades that will finish in-the-money.

Binary Option Trading Signals

Call or Put?

Binary options trading signals are buy and sell recommendations which are delivered to traders by a third party by means of alerts. These alerts are generated to assist traders with identifying the best opportunities for profit, hence, a trader who follows these suggestions will be able to trade more successfully.

There are many specialist companies that offer trading signals to binary option traders. These companies have professional traders working behind the scenes, constantly analysing various fundamental, technical, and economic influences that can impact the price of an asset in order to identify trends and spot opportunities, which they then share with their clients in order to execute a successful binary option trade. Trading signals provided by these companies are usually sent out daily via email or SMS/Text message and will include information on the asset e.g. gold, Apple, S&P 500, the entry price i.e. the market price that you should enter the trade at, the market direction, telling you whether to select CALL or PUT and the expiry time needed for the trade. Many trading signal providers will also provide a detailed summary of their previous signals and how they performed, so that traders can check the accuracy of the provider for themselves.

Trading signals providers such as world-class Trading Central, used for predictions on future price movements, generally offer monthly subscriptions to their service. Some of these offer trial periods so you can test out their service to see if it's right for you. The way they work, typically, is that you will receive a text message or email one or more times per day with the exact information you need to make a profitable binary options trade. The information sent to you will look something like this:

Signal for 25/11/14 – Call – Nasdaq -2642 – 18:00 GMT

This signal is telling you to purchase a CALL option for the asset Nasdaq when the market price is at 2642 or lower. In this case, 18:00 GMT is the expiry time to set on the trade. You then take this information to your preferred binary option platform and execute a trade using the parameters given.

It is important not to expect a 100% success rate on the signals provided. Although these services give you a much higher probability of winning a binary options trade, a 90-100% success rate is never guaranteed. A 70-80% success rate is much more realistic to achieve. You must already have an account with a binary option broker before you can put these signals into use.

Binary Option Robots

How to Benefit with Binary Options Robots?

A binary options trading robot is basically a piece of software that is capable of accurately analyzing data that might impact the way in which assets' price moves. It has both manual and automated mode. The only difference between them is that users can customize their investment settings according to their very own preferences and place the trades themselves when choosing the first or let the system do everything on their behalf if they pick the latter.

How to Get Started in a few Easy Steps?

Sign Up: Usually, only a couple of basic details have to be entered into the registration form: name, email address and telephone number. Users can choose a binary options trading system from the reputable ones

Register a robot account

Start trading and collect profits

Fund trading account

$250 is the minimum amount to start. You can withdraw It anytime.

Switch auto-trading ON

The software will start trading the financial markets online.

Collect profits

Withdrawal requests are typically fulfilled in 2 working days.

➽ Choose a Broker: Each online investment robot works with different brokerages. After signing up with a given software a confirmation letter is sent almost immediately to the trader's inbox. Traders are then required to decide which brokerage would they like to work with.

➽ Withdrawal Procedure: Most robots offer expedited or instant withdrawals. In order to receive their earnings, investors have to fill out a request form and apply a copy of personal ID for verification.

The most common binary options robot software is an auto trading system that executes trades automatically in your user account. These actions are based on a combination of investment styles and signals over which you have a certain degree of limited control. These online platforms can be signal providers and auto-traders at the same time.

Why Opt for Binary Options Robots?

There are many income generating solutions available in the vast spaces of the Internet. Some users may ask themselves why should they go and pick exactly binary options automated systems.

There are many reasons why traders should do this. Let's mention a couple of them here:

- **Guaranteed Profits:** One of the best things about binary options investment robots is that the odds for losing financial operations are almost eliminated. This does not mean that they can not happen, but most systems have either risk-level control or stop-loss features.
- **100% Free of Charge:** There is absolutely no fee that one has to place in order to trade online using this type of profit amplifying solutions. Sign up and registration are completely free. This is one of the great things about binary options.
- **Everybody Trades Binary Options:** They have become so popular that there is almost not a single person on the Internet who has not tested them. Which is good because there is lots of feedback about the performance of particular systems. It is also one more reason to try them – if everybody does, then they must be profitable.
- **No Skills Required:** Users are not obliged to have any formal education or professional training in or-

der to get started and acquire solid profits. The greater part of profit amplifying solutions have a fully automated mode which enables traders to just sit back and relax as the software does everything for you.

- **Provided Guidance & Support:** One of the great benefits of getting started with a binary options online platform is that if investors desire to acquire additional information and knowledge, they have the opportunity to do so. Most legit income generating solutions have interactive learning materials available for free. Customer support service is also a must.

How to Choose the Best Binary Options Robot?

There are several key factors which users should be on the lookout for when considering to open an account with a given binary options automated software. Even if one is not an expert, he should at least read a couple of reviews that are available on the Internet. A simple search should lead him or her to the answer they need.

Another thing which is good to be always on the lookout for are the special features that the binary options trading system of your personal choosing has. Presence of available educational materials, reliable 24/7 customer support and an automated mode that is capable of placing just the right investments instead of the user.

You should always rely on the opinion of other users. Generally, if a large group of people hold a certain regard of a particular income generating platform, then they must be on the right track. Especially, if they have been losing their initial investments and not accumulating any returns. Also, if investors are satisfied with the way it works – it means that it is legit and not part of the scam products.

Here are the Robot providers our readers prefer best:

Binary Options Robot:
http://host.robotclicks.com/click.php?project_id=Wb&affiliate_id=Kt&affiliate_display=Kt

http://host.robotclicks.com/click.php?project_id=Wb&affiliate_id=Kt&affiliate_display=Kt&lp=Nb

Traders's Budy:
http://host.robotclicks.com/click.php?project_id=Jbn-&affiliate_id=Kt&affiliate_display=Kt

Understanding Binary Trading Strategies

Binary option trading requires the use of strategies to get started. In much the same way as you use a trading strategy with the stock market, so it is with binary options. The point of using strategies is to gain a competitive edge in the market. When investors speak of binary trading strategies, they are essentially talking about fundamental analysis and technical analysis. Various other strategies are employed throughout, including the Martingale Strategy, Bollinger Bands and MACD, the Straddle Strategy, the Hedging Strategy, the Reversal Binary Options Strategy, 60 Second Trading Strategies, Bully Trading System, and more.

When you trade binary options, you can expect *in the money* profits of 70% to 90%, or more. There are 4 general asset categories to trade, including stocks, indices, commodities and currencies. And since expiry times range from as little as 60 seconds to several weeks in duration, you can generate profits in double-quick time. Before you begin trading binary options, it's important to stay abreast of the effects of strategy and risk management. Staying in the loop as it pertains to financial news updates is important with binary options trading too. Fortunately, binary options (digital options) either finish in the money or out of the money. It should be understood that certain brokers will offer cash back on losing trades, but that is typically limited to 10% of the trade amount.

How to Trade Binary Options with Fundamental Analysis

Traders who have a keen interest in the economics of binary options – the number crunching – will instantly be drawn to fundamental analysis. This method of trading relies on the market fundamentals to anticipate future price movements. During the 2008 global crisis, markets were sharply revised downwards and the fundamental analysis at the time supported such a downward revision. But fundamental analysis is not limited to major market movements or events; it also includes daily data such as inflation rates, unemployment rates, non-farm payroll, interest rates, etc. This information is made available through economic calendars at the top binary options brokers and other reputable sites.

How to Trade Binary Options with Technical Analysis

Traders who enjoy using charts will find technical analysis much to their liking. By studying the exchange rates of charts and other technical analysis tools (candlestick charts, digital info), traders attempt to gauge the future direction of asset price movement. The theory of chart analysis is predicated on the notion that past trading patterns imprint on the market. As a result, the market tends to remember what has previously occurred. By carefully analyzing the past behaviour of the markets it is possible to make educated forecasts as to the future possibilities in the market. This is especially helpful as it relates to exchange rates in currency pairs, stock price movements, indices, and commodities. Various technical indicators are available to assist in identifying trends and patterns vis-à-vis market behaviour.

Making Binary Trading Strategies Work for You

Becoming a success story with binary options trading is no mean feat. It requires hard work, insight and due diligence. Even with the best available insights, there is no sure-fire way to success in binary options trading. For starters, one of the best binary trading strategies is to trade assets that you understand. This could range from currency pairs like USD/EUR, GBP/USD to indices, stocks, and commodities. Risk minimization includes not investing everything in a single trade, or a handful of trades, and not investing too much capital. The golden rule for binary trading strategies is to limit your overall exposure to 5% of your capital. For a trading account of $2,000 the maximum trade on any one position should be limited to $100. And it is also ill advised to place trades on multiple assets that will all be in the money only if they move in the same direction.

Call & Put Options

Successful traders have a winning mindset. The psychological aspect of trading necessitates that traders understand how to trade and how not to trade. It is foolhardy to chase losses in binary options trading and it makes precious little sense to invest more than 5% of your capital on any individual trade. These rules are in place to protect your capital and your overall wellbeing. The absence of emotion in your daily trading regimen bodes well for your long-term success. The urgency of trying to force a winning outcome only leads to further losses. In all instances, the golden rules for trading binary options are clear: use fundamental analysis and technical analysis to the best of your ability. Despite the analysis, the fundamentals of binary options trading are simple: place a put option if you believe the asset price will fall below the strike price at expiry time, or a call option if you believe the asset price will rise above the strike price at expiry time.

Trading Strategies

Basically, there are countless strategies to trade with, most of the standard strategies you can find in the following chapters of this book.

I myself have the following strategy:

1. I am trading exclusively with the following assets: EUR/USD, gold, silver and oil.

2. At the beginning of the trading session I will look and inform myself of the latest financial reports on these 4 assets.

3. Then I will set the chart this way that I can follow the chart of the last 12, 8 and 4 hours. And then I decide on the basis of this chart whether the general long-term trend is a PUT or CALL option on this asset.

4. I am trading only in 10-15 minutes Trades

5. Follow the chart closely and every time you see at the

chart that a relatively large difference has occurred to the active Trend than place your Trade.

6. End your trading session as soon you have reached your set goals.

7. Align yourself to this following trading plan

8. Trade this strategy first with a demo account or with low capital, so you get a feeling for the strategy.

Trading Plan

Daily profit / loss limit:	always 10% of the total trading capital
Previously maximum trades per session:	74
Average earnings at 1000 Trades:	25% per session
Highest loss at 1000 Trades: -	minus 10.00%
Losses generally at 1000 Trades:	2 Total losses each with 10% and -8% per session

Trading-Plan:

Capital:	500 Euro	
Daily Limits:	+/- 50 Euro	+/- 20 Euro
Investment per trade:	10 Euro	5 Euro

Capital:	1.000 Euro	
Daily Limits:	+/-100 Euro	+/- 50 Euro
Investment per trade:	20 Euro	10 Euro

Capital:	2.500 Euro	
Daily Limits:	+/-250 Euro	+/- 125 Euro
Investment per trade:	50 Euro	25 Euro

Capital:	5.000 Euro	
Daily Limits:	+/- 500 Euro	+/- 250 Euro
Investment per trade:	100 Euro	50 Euro

Capital:	10.000 Euro	
Daily Limits:	+/- 1.000 Euro	+/- 500 Euro
Investment per trade:	200 Euro	...100 Euro

Capital:	50.000 Euro	
Daily Limits:	+/- 5.000 Euro	+/- 2.500 Euro
Investment per trade:	1.000 Euro	500 Euro

Capital:	100.000 Euro	
Daily Limits:	+/- 10.000 Euro	+/- 5.000 Euro
Investment per trade:	2.000 Euro	1.000 Euro

The figures on the right side are 50% of the normal tradings. This is for traders who want to minimize the risk.

Trading Guidelines

Binary options trading may look simpler and the payouts comparatively easier to learn than in other markets, but the truth is that if the binary options trading guidelines are not followed, the trader will run into severe problems and lose money faster than the speed of sound.

So what are the binary options trading guidelines that every intending participant in the binary options market should follow?

1. The fact that there are many financial assets to trade and many trade types does not mean that the trader should trade everything tradable. It is better to master one or two trade types and just a few financial assets than to be a Jack of All Assets and master of none.
2. Risk management is something that should be close to a trader's heart when trading any financial market and binary options is no exception. Some traders try to aim for returns of up to 800% in a single day by opening multiple positions, hoping to strike it big with all of them. This is a wrong approach. Rather, open positions in such a way that your risk exposure

is never more than 5% of your account size. For instance, if you use a chart pattern for a trade which you are sure will be a winner, place two trades around it. If you use a rising wedge to predict that an asset will head to the downside, you can use a FALL or DOWN trade as well as a NO TOUCH trade with an upside target. This way, the trader can kill two birds with a single stone.

3. One key binary options trading guideline that many traders frequently disobey is to have a trading plan. A trader who is trading to make money to spend for the weekend and someone saving for a business he intends to start two years down the road will not have the same trading style. Your plan will determine your goal, and how you want to get to your goal. If you are a trader with a long term goal, it is better to reduce risk and compound your profits over time, which will require discipline.
4. Stick to the optimal trading times. It is bad practice to stay up late at night when you should be sleeping and giving your body the best kind of weapon to recuperate for the rigors of the next day. Not only will your brain be tired at that time of the day, you rob your body of the ability to function properly the next day. So all the next day's trades will stand the chance of being jeopardized as well.

5. In the same vein, some assets are best traded at certain times of the day. A stock index asset can only be traded when the parent market is open, and currency assets will only have maximum volatility during the overlapping time zones. These are the best times to trade.

If traders follow these guidelines, they might make bankable profits from this adventure.

Here are some personal tips for your trading:

1. Always trade with only 2% of the total available capital per option. Risk management is also important here!

2. Enter your PUT or CALL order shortly before the expiry of the option into the system.

3. Focus on a maximum of four assets and never make more than 5 trades simultaneously.

4. If you find no reasonable Setup waive the trade, every hour comes a new opportunity.

5. Avoid overtrading, set clear goals how much you want to win a day and take the profits also consistently with. Each trading day presents new opportunities!

6. As a novice in trading do not place any 60SEC TRADES!

7. Never capitalize your trades! Always put the same amount per trade and do not capitalize it at a loss

8. Limit your sessions to 60-80 trades per session.

9. Make no more than 2 sessions per trading day!

10. As a novice do not trade on different broker platforms at the same time!

11. Trade only at major trading hours (in Europe between 8.00am and 12.00am)

12. Do not capitalize your trades continuously upwards and draw in intervals 50% of your total capital back to your banking account and out of trading.

Bullish or Bearish Strategies

One of the main advantages of binary options trading over the traditional stock market lies in the fact that binary options can be traded profitably in both bullish and bearish markets. A bullish market arises when the prices of many assets follow an ascending path, denoting high activity and interest. A bearish market, on the contrary, occurs when asset prices fall over a period of time, denoting the growing hesitation of investors, or a sell-off prior to a foreseen decline. Understanding why assets perform in certain ways, and the factors that create uptrends and downtrends in price values, can help you correctly apply bullish or bearish strategies, leading to successful trades.

Analyzing Market Trends

There are three main indicators that can help you decide whether to apply bullish or bearish strategies, and predict evolution of market trends: technical analysis, fundamental analysis, and market sentiment.

Technical Analysis: Technical analysis looks at graphs and charts to view the current market situation and its evolution over time. Once the current trend has been determined, the main thing you need to consider is the highest and lowest realised values of the asset (known as resistance and support levels) in order to determine how much longer the price may continue to move in the same direction.

Fundamental Analysis: Fundamental analysis focuses on external events, such as economic news and important financial data releases that can affect the price of assets. In the application of bullish and bearish strategies for trading binary options, market news plays an essential role as strong indicators of market movements, and many traders time their trades specifically around them for more increased profits.

Market Sentiment: Market sentiment is primarily employed in combination with fundamental analysis and looks at the general feeling of investors towards the market. If investors are feeling hesitant, and shy away from trading despite a somewhat bullish market for example, the trend can quickly turn bearish if no other events are brought to consider on the issue.

As bullish and bearish strategies deal with general trends in the market and follow major financial news releases, they can be quite easy to use even by the novice trader who has not yet mastered more complicated strategies. The bullish and bearish strategies, moreover, do not apply only to overall markets but can be successfully used for trading specific assets as well. When the market turns bearish, for example, investors are likely to flock to specific safe-haven assets in order to protect their investments, or offset some of the risks of the market at least, creating bullish conditions for those specific assets. On the options trading platforms you can follow the bullish or bearish trends on many different assets that will help you determine market conditions and the appropriate strategy to apply to your trades.

60 Seconds Trade Strategy

How It Works?

Binary Options Trading is generally known for its short expiry dates, usually within several minutes to a few hours, which offer quick trades with high returns. One particular binary options trade, however, beats even these speedy expiry times: the 60 Seconds Trading Platform. As the name suggests, this platform offers trades that automatically expire after a minute. Although one has to be extremely quick to enter these trades (since even a few seconds can make a big difference) trading 60 seconds options appeals to many traders as it offers more trading opportunities, especially when the market is generally slow. It can also lead to quick profits. As with all trading, however, you should not enter the market haphazardly, but approach your investments with a specific strategy that can stabilize your success rate in the long run.

The 60 Seconds Trade Strategy relies on placing repeated trades of the same monetary value at a high frequency that allow you to capitalize on short, yet sudden, price movements. When you log on to a 60 seconds trading platform you need to monitor the movement of the asset's value on a minute chart. Watching the price closely will enable you to observe the price's micro-movements, thus catching patterns that would be lost to traders watching the price move on larger time scales. As you observe the chart you should try to establish the pattern's support and resistance points which will help you decide the best time to begin your trades. You can also consult pivot point charts which show the range of a value's daily movements in order to clarify your position.

When the value of your asset reaches a pivot point, either a resistance or a support line, you have to be ready to start placing your trades. If the price reaches, or better yet surpasses, its daily resistance line, for example, the moment it begins to drop back down you need to place as many "put" trades as possible, until you see the price either nearing its support lever or otherwise turning in a definitive way. Although not all your trades may finish in-the-money, the majority of them will if you catch the trend on time, leaving you with an overall profit.

The fast pace of the 60 Seconds Trading Strategy, which utilizes the short expiry dates of these trade to their maximum advantage, can be highly exciting and engaging as the trader needs to focus on following the value's micro-movements. You should never forget, however, that all trades carry certain risks with them, and that it is always better to trade with your logic, and not your emotions. The best way, to remain calm and logical during an exciting trading session is to go in armed with concrete strategies such as the one presented here that will help you finish in-the-money.

Index Scalping

We all know the basic rule of traditional trading: buy low, sell high. Index scalping follows this rule, but on a much smaller – miniscule almost – scale. When using the index scalping strategy an investor aims at making many small profits on slight price changes that eventually add up to sizeable amounts. But how exactly can you achieve this?

Index Scalping Strategy

Unlike a traditional investor, a scalper places anywhere between ten to a couple of hundred trades in a single day which he enters and exits within a short amount of time. The underlying notion of index scalping is that small movements in price values are easier to catch than large movements. Thus when scalping, you need to buy stocks at the bid price and quickly sell them just a few cents higher for a profit. The minute difference in price means that you need to buy and sell a lot of stocks and to make a lot of trades in a day to accumulate large overall gains, hence the high volume of trades placed by scalpers. This strategy also requires that you have a strict exit strategy of selling stocks as soon as a higher price is reached in order to prevent large losses that could eliminate the many small gains you make over a day's trading. Unlike a traditional trader who may have approximately an equal number of winning and losing trades, but with the winning ones of course returning greatly higher amounts than the amounts lost in the losing ones, a successful scalper will have a much higher ratio of winning to losing trades. That's because the profits of winning trades in scalping do not far exceed (if at all) the losses of losing trades, and overall profit depends entirely on a higher number of winning trades.

Benefits of Trading Indices

Index Trading can be quite tricky and requires not only a lot of time and effort in order to achieve a high volume of trades, but also good timing in catching the small movements of the market. Nevertheless, there are certain advantages to this strategy that make it appealing to scalpers.

Scalping trades receive very little exposure to the market as they are opened and closed within minutes, which lessens the probability of running into major events that can adversely and significantly affect the value of a price.

The small movement of a few cents that the scalper looks for in the market, occur much more easily than big movements of traditional trading. A big move signifies an imbalance in supply and demand which is hard to obtain, but a small difference of a few cents can occur for any minor reason.

Small movements occur not only more easily, but also at a much higher frequency. Even on a quiet day where markets are generally stable, a scalper can find many small movements to exploit for profit.

Commodities Online Trading Strategies

With the advent 24/7 global news, buying and selling commodities has become the most accessible and straightforward route for new traders to make money on the financial markets. Geopolitical events can have a direct and often immediate impact on commodity prices. Successful commodity traders keep a close eye on trusted news sources (Bloomberg, Reuters etc), analyze key global events, extrapolate probable outcomes, and execute timely and profitable trades.

Most online trading platforms offer their clients real-time price charts, access to breaking news, and technical analysis for all their tradable assets – everything they need to make informed commodity trades.

This wealth of information has allowed investors to spend less time on research as it is all done for them, and more time developing successful strategies.

Most Popular Commodities

OIL (BRENT CRUDE)

Major Producers / Exporters:

COUNTRY	% OF WORLD PRODUCTION
Russia	13%
Saudi Arabia	11%
United States	11%
Iran	5%
China	5%
**Canada*	4%
Iraq	4%
United Arab Emirates	3%
Mexico	3%
Kuwait	3%

**Oil is Canada's biggest export and is valued at US$90 billion per year. The US is Canada's largest trading partner and imports 2 million barrels of crude oil from Canada every day. This relationship, together with the fact that oil is denominated in US dollars gives rise to a close, or direct correlation between the prices of oil and the Canadian dollar. An informed binary options trade on a rising price of oil is a put option on the USD/CAD.*

1) Denomination

For over half a decade, oil has been bought and sold in US dollars. With the dollar less stable than it used to be, OPEC (Organization of the Petroleum Exporting Countries) is considering changing oil's denominated currency to the euro or a basket of multiple currencies. If this goes ahead, there is likely to be a short-term drop in the price of Brent Crude oil.

2) Alternative Hydrocarbon Sources

Extracting oil with wells and drilling platforms is not the only way to access valuable hydrocarbon products. Oil shale and tar sands contain vast quantities of oil. When these technologies mature and the price of production decreases they are certain to have a negative impact on the price of crude oil.

3) Green Energy

The burning of fossil fuels is now generally accepted as being a major cause of global warming. This has resulted in an increasingly aggressive push for 'greener' energy sources. If these alternative energy sources become economically viable, the price of oil will plummet.

GOLD

Major Producers / Exporters:

COUNTRY	**% OF WORLD PRODUCTION**
South Africa	14%
**Australia*	9%
United States	9%
Russia	8%
China	6%
Peru	6%
Canada	4%
Indonesia	4%
Uzbekistan	3%

**Australia is one of the world's biggest gold producers and its currency, the Australian dollar, shows a strong, direct correlation with the price of gold. However, investors should note that the correlation is unlikely to be stable for intra-day trades.*

1) Industrial Application

As well as being a precious metal, gold is used extensively in industry, particularly in the electronics sector. Gold is an extremely good electrical conductor and does not corrode or tarnish. It is therefore the ideal material for the contact points in solid state electronic devices which operate using very low voltages and currents.

2) Supply/Demand

Due to its high cost of production (approx. US$250 per ounce), it is estimated that the supply of gold will fail to meet demand within the next 45 years. Indeed, according to the World Gold Council, 2,500 metric tonnes of gold is mined annually, but total yearly consumption (jewelry, investment, industry etc.) is 3,500 metric tonnes.

3) Economic Health

Gold has always been considered a safe haven among investors, and should be thought of as a currency that cannot be influenced by the monetary policies of individual nations. Hence, in times of economic strife, investors turn to gold as a hedge against inflation.

Tips to Rule Your Trade

There are several basic trading rules for people who are trading binary options. These rules are simple and straightforward and are there to make your trading experience profitable.

The first rule that you should follow even before thinking about transacting a trade is to conduct due diligence on the trade you are thinking of doing. This means that you should research facts about the asset. Never ever trade on gut feelings. The reason for deciding whether to trade high because the assets price will move higher or trade low because the asset price will move lower should be based on what you can learn from technical analysis charts, or from reading the financial press, or from conducting some fundamental analysis of economic news and statistic.

The second rule is to just concentrate on a few assets to trade binary options with, rather than trade all types. Get to know the characteristics of the assets really well. Take one asset class and concentrate on that for a while until you get to understand it fully. Then go on to another asset class and learn that fully too. The more knowledge you have about an asset, the more you will understand why it is moving up and why it is moving down. Also, try to understand the positive and negative links between asset classes and within asset classes. There are currencies which are linked to commodities either positively (they both move the same way) or negatively (they move in the opposite direction). There are also currencies which are linked to other currencies in the same way. It pays to learn the characteristics of these links and use this knowledge for trading.

Rule number three is, how you manage your money. You should always have a plan and know how much money you are willing to risk on each trade, or risk in a day. By planning carefully you can make money through online.

Rule number four is all about strategy. You should always have a plan when you are trading binary options. If you decide for example that a particular commodity will continue in an upward trend, because all the analysis you have done points to a particular plan, keep to it, even if you lose a trade because for a few hours there was a 'bounce' in the market. If your plan is sound the upward trend will continue after the small hiccup. The same applies for downward trends too. Of course if the market trend changes from that which you are following you should adapt your plan and change your own plan accordingly.

The final rule is the most crucial to a successful trading career. It is a logical progression to swimming in the shallow end before progressing to the deep end of the swimming pool. Most binary option brokers have demo accounts which you can use to practice your trading strategies on. Make sure you use them to get to know the trading platform, and to test out your trading plan and strategy. Remember that if you are not making money trading with a free demo account, there is no way you will make money trading with real money.

How to Trade Commodities like a Pro

Commodities are the new black!

In today's era of 24/7 news, it is easier than ever before for online traders to profit from the ups and downs of the commodity markets.

Historically, commodity trading took places in town markets. People would exchange the valuables or crops they owned for ones that they wanted, for example a farmer may have traded wheat for sugar or gold coins.

Test yourself on the examples below:

- A terrible drought in Brazil, the world's largest coffee bean grower, will reduce the global supply of coffee. Should you trade coffee up or down?
- Emerging economies such as China are continuing to industrialize and the growing middle class means an increase in demand for food supplies like sugar. Should you trade sugar up or down?
- Investments in water and wind energies are paying off and so the demand for oil is set to decrease. Should you trade oil up or down?

Here are the answers:

* Lower coffee supply ->higher coffee prices
* Higher demand for sugar -> higher sugar prices
* Lower demand for oil -> lower oil prices

4. Know the relationships between assets

By trading on a binary options platform, rather than a commodities-only exchange, you can take advantage of the strong relationships that exist between various commodities and other asset groups. So with just one bit of news and research, you can place two or three different trades, and increase your profit potential two or three times over. Consider oil. This is Canada's biggest export, and therefore when the price of oil goes up, so does the value of the Canadian dollar. An informed trader (like yourself) could place an up trade on oil as well as a down trade on the USD/CAD. Remember here that the USD/CAD pair goes down when the CAD goes up.

With the above tips at the ready, it's time to start trading commodities. The beauty of commodity trading is that it really is accessible and rewarding. Just do your research and analysis correctly, and you should be good to go like a pro.

How to Trade Commodity Online

Trading commodities online is a simple process to get started and an appealing way to invest on the internet. As the commodity market gathers momentum, and interest in the market gains popularity, daily trading volumes are also increasing, which in turn leads to greater potential profits.

How to Get Started

The first thing you need to do is choose a commodity broker, most of which offer online trading. You will need to open an account and submit details of your financial information. This is important as commodities are highly leveraged and there is a chance you can lose more money than you invest. Therefore, a broker will want to know your income, net worth and credit worthiness before they decide whether they deem you an acceptable risk and suited to trade commodities, and agree to sign you up. The greater your income, trading experience and credit worthiness, the better chance you have for approval.

Once your account is approved for trading, you will have to fund it, but before you begin trading real money, it is advisable to have a well-researched trading plan in place and practice using the broker's demo account. This is an essential step towards mastering online commodity trading.

Trading through a demo account will help you understand the effects that leverage has on your risk capital, and discover what is comfortable for you. You will be able to use technical analysis tools to help you decide on exit and entry points in the commodities market without risking your own capital.

Some online commodity brokers also offer online courses and there are also books on online commodity trading which explain the various risk management instruments available to reduce your risk when trading commodities.

Trading commodities online appeals to many for a number of reasons. The benefit is that you virtually have everything at your fingertips when you log in to your trading account; most online brokers will have real time quotes, charts, news, technical analysis and research available for their clients. This has opened the door for many online traders to make more of their own trading decisions and implement trading strategies that once were not available to the average retail trader. The commissions are also much lower.

You do however need to be aware of two main issues facing online traders. Firstly, you may not have someone on hand to help you with your trades so you really need to make sure that you are well researched. In addition, the advent of online trading has accelerated the problem of over trading which has been an issue with commodity traders for decades. If you find yourself placing a flurry of trades and look back at the end of the day wondering what happened, you are overtrading.

Once you have mastered the commodity trading software, have become fairly proficient using some technical analysis and have decided on the level of risk capital and leverage you feel comfortable with, you are ready to switch from a demo account to a live trading account. Online commodity trading can be highly profitable if you proceed with a reputable broker such as 24 Option, who can offer you a flexible medley of services, allowing you to begin slowly and increase your trading level at your own pace as you gain confidence.

How to Invest in Major Indices?

An index is a measurement of the changes in a pool of stocks which represent a segment of the market. They tell us where the market is going and what the likely trend is. Investing in an index is a much easier and cheaper option than investing in every stock in the index itself. It would be very tedious to follow every single stock traded in a market so a small segment of the market is chosen that is as much as possible representative of the total market. In an ideal world any change in the price of an index mirrors an exact comparative change to the stocks which are in the index. Stock market indices are a very important feature of our daily financial news and it is important that the mechanics behind them are fully understood before you consider using the information from them for investment purposes.

Once you start following the markets, you will note that there are investment market trends that can be observed broadly in certain sectors of the stock market. Comprehending these market trends and knowing how to evaluate stock prices is vital. Stock Index trading values spanning the whole day are continuously recorded and an average taken at the end of each day. A comparison of these averages will give you a good idea as to the price movements of the stocks.

In the US there are three major indices: The Dow Jones Industrial Average, one of the most widely quoted of all the market indicators which consists of 30 of the largest publicly traded firms in the U.S., the Standard and Poor's 500 (S&P 500) containing the stocks of 500 Large-Cap corporations which comprises over 70% of the total market cap of all stocks traded in the U.S. and the NASDAQ Composite, a broad market index of all of the common stocks and similar securities traded on the NASDAQ stock market. Other major indices are the Nikkei 225, the stock market index for the Tokyo Stock Exchange, the UK FTSE 100 which contains 100 of the most highly capitalised companies traded on the London Stock Exchange and the DAX 30 which measures the performance of the 30 largest German companies.

As we have seen, stocks are components of the overall index so any movements either up or down in the value of the stock will likely change the price of the overall index. It follows therefore that a change in a stock price in an index with fewer components such as the DAX 30 will have a greater knock-on effect on the overall index value compared to that of a larger index like the S&P 500.

Understanding what influences prices can help you to determine the correct price direction when you are placing your trades. Remember that not all news will have an impact on the price of the stock and subsequently the index. What is important is how the trading community reacts to the news which is largely based on perceived impact.

One final point to remember is that following one index is not sufficient as it will not give the true picture of prevailing market status. It is recommended that you take into account the all major indices across all asset classes before making a decision about investing.

With a wealth of historical and current information on the major indices available on this platforms, you can confidently start trading indices with opportunities for sizeable profits.

How to Profit from Crude Oil

Crude oil is one of the most commonly traded commodities and is one of the most valued items in the world today. Without it, there would be no aviation or transportation and many businesses would come to a standstill or shut down.

The price of crude oil as a commodity soared during the first decade of the 21st century. If this period is any indication of what the future holds for oil, you will want to develop a winning game plan to take advantage and profit from this trend.

However, as the financial crisis struck Wall Street, Europe and the rest of the world markets, oil prices experienced an asset price deflation similar to what most other assets were experiencing worldwide. It is very important therefore to know what the fundamental influences on crude oil prices are as this will form the basis of your trading activities. These are the key factors:

- **Crude Oil Inventories Report:** This weekly report, released by the US Department of Energy, communicates the number of barrels of crude oil held in storage by commercial firms for the past week. The report is a reflection of whether the global crude stocks are rising or declining. This supply driven data will then affect the price of crude depending on market sentiment.

- **OPEC Quota:** The OPEC member countries contribute a significant quantity of crude oil to the global market, and fixing of quotas will ultimately determine supply and crude prices.
- **Weather Patterns:** You also need to watch seasonal weather changes. Extremely cold winters place more demand on heating oil, which is a by-product of crude oil. This will place a demand-driven upward pressure on crude prices.

Armed with this information, one of the first things that you should do if you want to trade crude oil is to gauge the market sentiment for the day. The price of crude oil is never a random event but rather a reflection of something going on somewhere in the world to influence the sentiment of traders towards the asset. Once sentiment is formed, the net positions of traders will determine whether the price of the asset will rise or fall.

The next step is to look for technical plays that will guide you to trade entries in the direction of the market sentiment. For instance, you may decide to use a chart pattern in evolution to either predict the price movement or predict an area where prices will likely head to in order to touch a specific price point. There are many strategies that can be employed and you should determine which one will be suited for your particular trade type. You also need to decide on what trade contract to trade on the binary options platform. The trade type will determine how the crude oil price movement will be played. Note that crude oil is not traded on a 24 hour basis. It is usually available for trading when the parent commodity markets are open for business. Your binary options broker will always indicate the times in which the asset can be traded.

Once you have all these factors in place, you can begin trading with a reputable broker such as 24 Option. Trading binary options is a cheaper and less risky way for you to trade than any other method and presents you with an excellent way to profit from crude oil.

How to Value a Stock

Valuing stocks can be a tricky business, and it has often been described as more of an art than a science. The value of a stock is not equivalent to its market price; stock valuation estimates how accurately the price of a stock reflects the company's (future) performance, and can vary as widely as individual investors' opinions and predictions. Simply put, the value of a stock is a combination of a company's current value and a projection of its future profits. A company, therefore, may have little actual value at present but have a high stock valuation owing to expected growth in the market. Buying stocks that promise great growth and increased profits in the future is the key to successful stock investment.

Stock Value

The basic tools for assessing the value of a stock are the valuation ratios. These ratios represent a company's share price to various aspects of the company's financial performance and are given in the format of: price/earning (P/E), price/sales (P/S), price/cash flow (P/CF), etc. Once you choose the valuation that most interests you regarding a specific company, you then have to decide whether its value is too high or too low. Not all investors will agree on this point and it is not uncommon for two people looking at the same numbers for the same company to arrive to different conclusions concerning the stock's value. But how do you decide if the value is too low or too high?

There are two basic methods of applying valuation ratios for determining the value of a stock. The most popular method is relative valuation, and it compares the stock's valuations with the valuations of other stocks in the same sector or with the company's own historical stock valuations. Keep in mind, however, that not all companies in a sector are created equal and comparing Toyota's shares, for example, to Cadillac's is not likely to give you a good gauge of either company's relative value. When using comparative valuation you need to research your stocks well and understand the factors that may justify the differences in their market price before making a decision on their value.

The second method for valuing stocks is absolute (also called intrinsic) valuation, and focuses only on fundamentals (such as dividends, cash flow, and growth rate) for a particular company, without comparisons to other companies. The most common way to estimate a company's absolute value is by calculating a company's current value of its future free-cash flows. Calculating absolute value can be challenging, because it is difficult to forecast how quickly a company's cash flows will increase, for how long they will keep increasing, and at what percentage of today's monetary value they should be calculated.

Valuing stock is not an easy business and they best way to go about it to study your stocks carefully and to include many different parameters in your calculations, just as you would do if you were investing your money in a new house or a new car rather than stocks.

How to Choose Assets to Trade

The binary options market has one great advantage over other financial markets in that the amount of movement in the price of an asset does not affect the final pay-out because the pay-out for binary options is the same, however much the price has moved. All the trader needs to do is determine the right asset to trade and also determine in which direction the price is going, and if, at the time of expiry, the price will be higher or lower than the entry price.

How can you determine the right asset to trade from the many diverse assets of stocks, currencies, commodities and indices? This decision is based on your knowledge of how specific types of assets behave under certain market conditions. Volatile markets are the best markets to trade as in volatile conditions assets move quickly up or down, whereas, in non-volatile market conditions, there are only a few assets that perform. You have to carefully evaluate the current market conditions to get the best results.

Probably the most volatile asset class is that of the foreign exchange market where currencies are traded. There are several currency pairs that are traded as binary options and the EUR/USD, NZD/USD and USD/JPY are the currency pairs that have the highest liquidity and therefore, are the most volatile. You could also trade the USD/CHF in the opposite direction to your EUR/USD trade as they are, generally speaking, negatively correlated. The best time to trade binary option currencies is while economic news is being released.

Binary options in commodities don't have the characteristics of binary options in currencies because the underlying assets like gold, oil and silver etc. are traded in the future. This has the effect of reducing volatility, however, if you watch the contract periods of the underlying asset you will find that commodity binary options are good to trade at the beginning part of a contract of a contract period.

There are many popular stocks that can be traded as binary options. Stocks such as IBM, Microsoft and Google are all affected by either economic news or by company reports. The best time to trade binary options in stocks is when the earnings of the particular company you wish to trade are reported, or after major news item about the company.

The Index markets are also very volatile and can be compared to the currency markets because in essence the index is a bundle of assets and not just one asset. Also, as they are electronic markets they are open 24 hours a day. Some indices take a while to respond to financial news or company reports. The best way to trade index binary options is to only trade the index when there is a major announcement about a stock or stocks within the index.

It is important that you understand the characteristics of asset classes of binary options in order to know what to do under different market conditions.

How Political Events Affect Stocks

Events Influence the Market

Company stock prices and the stock markets in general can be influenced by world events such as war, civil unrest and terrorism. These influences can be direct and indirect and they often occur in chain reactions. For example, the social uncertainty and fear generated by the terrorist attacks on September 11th 2001 affected markets directly as they caused many investors in the United States to trade less and to focus on stocks and bonds with less risk. Indirectly, you can expect the stocks of military equipment companies and weapons manufacturers to rise in value as a nation gears up for armed conflict due to increased demand.

War affects the value of assets above all else. Even the suggestion of a war in the Middle East is often enough for the price of crude oil to sky-rocket due to the region being such a major oil exporter. Oil and stocks have a negative correlation so rising oil prices due to political unrest usually signals falling stock prices, especially those stocks denominated in dollars and energy stocks.

It is perhaps not surprising that some economists point to a potential economic upside to war. War at times can kick-start a fledgling economy especially its manufacturing base when forced to concentrate its efforts on war time production. Think of the United States in World War II. The U.S.'s entry into the war following the attacks on Pearl Harbor almost instantly pulled the country out of the grips of the Great Depression. While there is historical precedent for this viewpoint, most would agree that an improved economy at the cost of human lives is not a choice most would be willing to make.

Other political events which can affect the stock markets are government elections. Elections impact on a country's currency and are viewed by traders as a case of potential political instability and uncertainty which typically equates to greater volatility in the value of a country's currency. Unplanned elections can wreak havoc on a currency especially in cases where upheaval among citizens results in protests and work stoppages for example. In most situations, the political instability will outweigh any positive anticipated outcomes from a new government in the short run and related currencies will usually suffer losses. In the long-term, however, basic valuation factors and principals will once again apply and currencies should settle at or around a rate indicative of the country's economic growth prospects.

Political events can therefore have a profound effect on stock markets and seasoned investors often take advantage of this volatility. While it is very difficult to plan for the unexpected in the markets during these unsettling times, an informed trader will be quicker to react to global events than one who is unsure of what moves to make in their wake. Researching relevant information and following the trends in times of political conflict or uncertainty will allow you to make quick, informed decisions regarding your trading activities so that you can ultimately maximize your profits. Investors hoping to profit in times of volatility can choose regulated binary options brokers as their first point of call.

Trading-Seminar

I also offer individual seminars via Skype conference where I will explain my own trading strategy as mentioned in this book and will teach you how to place trades in real time.

You only need a good internet connection and a Skype account as well as a trading account with IQ-Option so that we can trade on the same charts and signals. Further it is necessary that you will transfer the fee of 199 Euro for the one hour trading seminar to my bank or paypal account.

Money back guarantee

If you have suffered a loss at the end of the seminar, I will refund you at the end of the seminar the amount of 199 Euro online.

Should the trading seminar ends in a profit for you, the amount of 199 Euros remains with me as seminar fee. I think that will be a fair offer to you and you can see that I am completely convinced of my strategy. Also I do not want to become rich through seminars this seminar fee only compensate my time I have to spend with you.

For seminar registrations please contact me at the following E-mail address:

Trading-King@swissmail.com

Please let me know in your email the following information:

Name:

Date of birth:

Place of living:

Sykpe address:

Phone:

Day and time of the desired seminar:

(Please only ask for dates to the main trading hours in Europe between 8am up to 12am or 4pm clock to 7pm preferably trading hours in the morning!)

Once I've edited your inquiry, I will reply not later than 24 hours and will confirm your preferred date for a seminar or reshedule with you.

Loan Agreement

Alternatively, you can invest straight into Trading King Ltd. We offer a fixed yield of 8.5% p.a. on your invested amount into our company.

Here you have the advantage that you do not take any risk of any losses in trading since you are invested in our company itself and not in any trades. This offer is for investors who like to minimize their risk.

If you are interested, please send an e-mail and ask for our loan agreement.

Trading-King@swissmail.com

Top Investment

We want to significantly expand our company internationally. To this end, we are looking for a reliable partner in the form of an equity investment of EUR 1 million.

We generate above-average profits with our different range of products (no trading) and thus also a top return on your investment.

If you are interested, please contact us at the following e-mail address and request our detailed business plan:

tradingking@asia.com

Trading Results

Here are the trading results of the last couple of months before printing of this book:

September 2015		October 2015	
18/09/15	+/- 0%	01/10/15	+ 0%
21/09/15	+ 4%	02/10/15	+ 2%
22/09/15	+ 4%	05/10/15	+ 2%
23/09/15	+ 6%	06/10/15	+ 2%
24/09/15	+5.5%	07/10/15	+ 2%
25/09/15	+ 6%	08/10/15	+ 2%
28/09/15	+ 5%	09/10/15	+ 7%
29/09/15	+ 4%	12/10/15	+2.5%
30/09/15	+ 5%	13/10/15	+ 2%
TOTAL:	+ 39.5%	TOTAL:	+ 21.5%

November 2015		December 2015	
05/11/15	+ 4%	01/12/15	+ 3%
16/11/15	+ 3.5%	02/12/15	+ 2%
17/11/15	+ 4%	03/12/15	+ 3%
19/11/15	+ 2%	04/12/15	+ 2.5%
24/11/15	+ 4%	07/12/15	+ 2.5%
30/11/15	+ 4%	08/12/15	+ 2%
		16/12/15	+ 9%
TOTAL:	+ 21.5%	17/12/15	+ 6.5%
		TOTAL:	+ 30.5%

January 2016		**February 2016**	
13/01/16	+ 6%	08/02/16	+ 5.5%
15/01/16	- 20%	10/02/16	+ 2%
18/01/16	+ 17%	11/02/16	+ 2%
19/01/16	+ 5%	12/02/16	+ 1%
20/01/16	+ 7%	16/02/16	+ 7%
		17/02/16	+ 2%
TOTAL:	+ 15%	23/02/16	+ 2.5%
		25/02/16	+ 2%
		TOTAL:	+ 24%

March 2016

01/03/16	+ 2%
02/03/16	+ 2%
09/03/16	+ 1.5%
10/03/16	+ 2%
11/03/16	+ 1%
14/03/16	+ 2%
15/03/16	+ 3%
16/03/16	+ 3%
17/03/16	+ 3%
TOTAL:	+ 19.5%

April 2016

04/04/16	+ 2.5%
05/04/16	+ 3.5%
06/04/16	+ 1.5%
07/04/16	+ 2%
08/04/16	+ 1.5%
11/04/16	+ 1%
12/04/16	+ 2%
13/04/16	+/- 0%
15/04/16	+ 2%
18/04/16	- 21%
19/04/16	+ 2%
20/04/16	+ 3.5%
22/04/16	+ 1%
26/04/16	+ 2%
TOTAL:	+ 3.5%

May 2016

09/05/16	+ 2%
13/05/16	+ 2%
18/05/16	+ 2%
20/05/16	+ 2%
23/05/16	- 3%
24/05/16	+ 5%
TOTAL:	+ 10%

As you can see, the trades of recent days and months are almost constant with a one day score of at least 2% profit. An excellent result, especially when compared to current capital market yields this is highly attractive!

The Lenormand Strategy

For a long time I have also been working together with author Derek Barclay, who published his book "Binary Options – My success with the Lenormand Strategy " with the same publisher as me. Derek Barclay created with his Lenormand Strategy for many years successfully stock market forecasts and has changed his forecasts from the stock market to binary options. After seeing many of his trading protocols of recent months, I am absolutely convinced of the accuracy of the forecasts and I decided to work together with Derek Barclay.

The high success rate of the forecasts has convinced me. Certainly there are not a lot of people who are connecting this cards and charts in one forecast together. This method is based exclusively on the long-term trading experience of the author in combination with the prediction of a Lenormand card set that is interrogated before the trade is placed. The author has been producing stock market forecasts for over 10 years with Lenormand cards.

Daily Forecast

The author creates a daily forecast for the following assets:

- Gold
- Silver
- Oil
- EUR / USD

The forecast refers to a daily trade starting at 10:00 am and closing at the end of the day.

The forecast will be sent to the subscriber by mail or Skype until at the latest 11:00 am on any commercial day (not Sat / Sun or Holidays). The monthly forecast can only be based on charts with a broker provided by the author. The VIP-Prognosis is a live day forecast and is available on 15 assets of your choice at a broker of your choice.

Monthly subscription of a daily forecast 149.90 Euro

VIP forecast 399.00 Euro

More information can be found on our website:

www.trading-king.hk

If you are interested in a monthly subscription or a VIP forecast, please ask for our terms and conditions at:

Trading-king@swissmail.com

Disclaimer

The present text has been prepared with great care. Nevertheless, errors cannot be completely ruled out. The author therefore takes no legal responsibility and no liability for damages resulting from the use of this book. In particular, the author has no obligation to replace any damages whatsoever resulted out of action taken by the reader in connection with this book. Readers of this book, we would like to express and to point out that no guarantee of success or similar guarantees can be given at anytime. Also no responsibility or any kind of consequences can be taken to the author by readers in connection with the contents of this book. The reader is responsible for all resulting ideas and actions comming out of this book.

Risk Warning

Binary Options and Contracts for Difference ('CFDs') are complex financial products, the trading of which involves significant risks. Binary Options trading may result in the loss of your investment whilst CFDs trading, which are marginal products, may result in the loss of your entire deposits. Remember that leverage in CFDs can work both to your advantage and disadvantage. Traders of Binary Options and CFDs do not own, or have any rights to, the underlying assets. Trading Binary Options and/or CFDs is not appropriate for all investors. Past performance does not constitute a reliable indicator of future results. Future forecasts do not constitute a reliable indicator of future performance. Before deciding to trade, you should carefully consider your investment objectives, level of experience and risk tolerance. You should not deposit more than you are prepared to lose. Please ensure you fully understand the risk associated with the product envisaged and seek independent advice, if necessary.

Zeitfracht Medien GmbH
Ferdinand-Jühlke-Straße 7
99095 Erfurt, Deutschland
produktsicherheit@kolibri360.de